FLORIDA DMV DRIVERS PERMIT TEST

370 written test Questions and Answers

By John D. Collyman

Copyright page

Disclaimer

The book is projected to be a general guide, to raise consciousness, and to aid people in making knowledgeable decisions in the context of their need.

The author takes no responsibility for any damage or injury, be it personal or monetary, as a result of the use or abuse of the information in this book.

Table of Contents

Chapter One: **Introduction**

Driving could be easy and fun if you know how to use the control elements in the vehicle, from the feet control pedals to the hand brake, steering wheels and gear. These are the basic elements that must be understood before one can talk about driving. The ability to drive and be looking at both the internal rear-mirror and the external side mirrors are vital before driving on the road.

The most notable attribute of driving is that it saves us a lot of time, which could have been spent waiting for a bus to arrive at the bus stop or the pick and drop of passengers by buses. Compare the above with determining a suitable time for your trip and planning to suit your schedule. After the planning, you can move into your vehicle and drive to your destination while managing any delay that could have taken place earlier

By and large, driving is an experience many would cherish to have. For that, the demand for a driver's license is a never-ending trend because every generation needs to have that unique experience. The fear, anxiety, and expectation all sum up, put the would-be driver into that level of ecstasy

With all the thrills and expectations, the Department of Motor Vehicle is there to ensure that drivers are safe and other road users are also safe. The life of nobody should be endangered due to unqualified drivers on the road.

The department conducts both theory and practical tests on intending drivers to test their readiness to drive on the road. These written test could be tough for one that is not prepared for the test. We have compiled three hundred and seventy questions with related past questions to prepare you for the theory test. The different topics from the handbook have been handled in the questions, with answers that will guide and assist even at the event of your practical test.

Reading to remember, and allowing what has been read to assimilate is essential. Due to this, candidates should read this book more than ones to create that required awareness, retention, and understanding.

Chapter Two: Safe Driving and Alcohol

1) **Your seat belt has both a lap belt and the shoulder belt. Which should you use?**

   A. Lap belt

   B. Shoulder belt

   C. Both the lap belt and shoulder belt

   D. As it pleases you

Answer = C

2) **There is a flashing amber traffic light at an intersection. What are you to do when you arrive there?**

   A. Drive straight before it turns red

   B. Stop and wait for the light to turn green

   C. Slow down and be careful before crossing

   D. Stop and yield to all traffic before crossing the intersection

Answer = C

3) There is an accident with little damage to the vehicle but no injury to anyone. What should you do?
   A. Leave your vehicles at the spot until a law enforcement officer arrives
   B. If possible, move your cars away from the traffic lanes
   C. Don't attempt to move the cars
   D. Barricade the scene

Answer = B

4) Backing your vehicle is always dangerous in the following vehicles?
   A. Cars
   B. Lorries
   C. Buses
   D. All of the above

Answer = D

5) What is the Blood Alcohol Concentration (BAC) level for a driver under 21 years old?
***

A. 0.04%

B. 0.03%

C. 0.02%

D. 0.01%

Answer = D

6) Riding at the back of a pickup truck is not allowed even when there are secured seats and approved safety belts

A. True

B. False

Answer = B

7) What is the speed limit for entry a dangerous intersection where visibility is not possible until you are too close to the junction?

A. Ten MPH

B. Fifteen MPH

C. Twenty MPH

D. Twenty-five MPH

Answer =B

8) **Which of the following is not an effect of alcohol?**

   A. It slows down reaction time

   B. It affects your judgment

   C. It improves concentration

   D. It reduces alertness

Answer = C

9) **What is a chemical test used for?**

   A. The measure alertness

   B. To test glucose level in the blood

   C. Th measure the alcohol content in the blood

   D. To check the vision of the driver

Answer = C

10) When you take some alcohol, and over the counter drugs, the combination can multiply the effect of the alcohol.

   A. True
   B. False

Answer = A

11) If you drive under the influence of alcohol, you will not be imprisoned, fined, or your license revoked?

   A. True
   B. False

Answer = B

12) What is the consequence of not taking a blood alcohol concentration test?

   A. Your car will be impounded
   B. Evidence will not be available
   C. Your driver's license will be revoked
   D. You can choose to perform another test

Answer = C

13) **You will be going for a social function where you are sure you will take some alcohol. How will you plan your coming back?**

   A. Have a ready-made coffee to take after the event
   B. Take a 30 minutes nap before leaving
   C. Reduce your alcohol intake in the event
   D. Go with a friend who does not drink alcohol

Answer = D

14) **You are on a non-prescription drug. What should you do before going on a trip?**

   A. Take the drug before driving
   B. Drive half-way the journey
   C. Read the label on the drugs before driving
   D. Sleep a minimum of two hours before driving

Answer = C

15) **Alcohol and drug mixture:**

A. Increases the potency of the drug

B. Increases the effect of the alcohol

C. Increases the impact of alcohol and drug

D. None of the above

Answer = C

16) **You took a cup of coffee after taken some alcohol. How will the coffee improve your state?**

A. It reduced the effect of the alcohol

B. It improves the blood level

C. It eliminates the alcohol level in the blood

D. It does not have any effect on the blood alcohol content

Answer = D

17) **You have finished taken some alcohol. Which of the following will be affected?**

A. Vision

B. Alertness

C. Judgment

D. All of the above

Answer = D

18) **Which of the following drugs will affect your driving coordination?**
   A. Cocain
   B. Marijuana
   C. Cough drugs
   D. All of the above

Answer = D

19) **Alcohol influence in the body is affected by:**
   A. Quantity of alcohol
   B. Bodyweight
   C. The amount of food eaten
   D. All of the above

Answer = D

20) **A breathalyzer is used to test for Blood Alcohol Content (BAC) in the body.**
   A. True

B. False

21) **As you drive under the influence of alcohol, you no longer have:**

   A. poor judgment
   B. proper coordination
   C. bad concentration
   D. poor vision

22) **You need to join the highway safely. Which of the following is the best way to join the traffic flow?**

   A. Allow for a significant gap in the traffic flow before speeding up quickly
   B. Gradually join the traffic flow on the side until a gap is available
   C. Join the traffic flow while flagging down other vehicles on the highway

D. Achieve a cruising speed on the ramp before joining the traffic on the highway

Answer = A

23) **You are to cross a railroad track with no rail crossing sign. What should you do?**

A. Ensure you can cross through without obstruction

B. Gradually edge forward to check for a train before crossing

C. Not pass any vehicle in your front at the crossing

D. All of the above

Answer = D

24) **You are driving at night. If you need to be sure of your safety, you must ensure to stop:**

A. Within seven seconds after braking

B. Within the distance that your headlight lighted

C. Within a safe distance, illuminated by your hazard light

D. None of the above

Answer = B

25) **You arrived at a railway track crossing. If the railway crossing bars have just been dropped down, what should you do?**

A. Go round the bar and proceed

B. Edge forward gradually to be sure the train is not near before crossing

C. Stop until the train has passed

D. Ensure that there is no vehicle on the track before you cross

Answer = C

26) **Which of the following age bracket is permitted to transport or possess alcohol?**

A. Below 18 years old

B. Above 18 years old

C. Below 21 years old

D. Above 21 years old

Answer = D

27) **You are under 21 years old. If you get convicted for driving under the influence of alcohol, what would be your sentence as a first time offender?**

A. One year vehicle license suspension

B. 500 dollar fine

C. Six-month of vehicle license suspension

D. Three months of vehicle license suspension and a 500 dollars fine

Answer = B

28) **A man refused to take the alcohol test. What is the penalty for the refusal? *****

A. Five hundred dollar fine

B. Suspension of driver's license or revocation

C. One month drug counseling clinic at an approved center

D. Six months of probation

Answer = B

29) **You were driving, and a police officer stops you, you should?**

   A. Pull over and use your hazard light

   B. Pull over, stay in your vehicle and put your hands on the steering wheel

   C. Pull over, get down from the vehicle and wait for the officer

   D. Pull over, get out of the vehicle, and walk over to the officer.

Answer = B

30) **You are under 21 years old and caught with an alcoholic beverage in your car. Which of the following is correct? *****

   A. Your vehicle may be impounded for three months

   B. You may lose your license for one year

   C. You may be fine $1000

   D. All of the above

Answer = A

31) You are under a DUI probation. What is the maximum allowable Basic Alcohol Concentration (BAC) while you are driving a vehicle? ***

A. 0.01%

B. 0.02%

C. 0.05%

D. 0.08%

Answer = A

32) How long will a DUI conviction remain on the driving record of a driver?***

A. One year

B. Three years

C. Seven years

D. Ten years

Answer = D

33) If your ability to drive is impaired, which of the following will not be the least likely cause of the impairment?

A. Use of overdose drugs

B. Taking hard drugs

C. Resting too much

D. Use of sedative medications

Answer = C

34) **A driver under 21 years old was stopped and tested for Blood Alcohol Concentration (BAC). If the test shows 0.04%, what should the officer do? *****

A. He should arrest the driver and suspend his license

B. He should make the driver do community service

C. Inform the insurance company of the driver

D. Inform the driver's relatives

Answer = A

35) **You have consented for Blood Alcohol Concentration test (BAC) if you:*****

A. Are born in Florida

B. Drive in Florida

C. Live in Florida

D. Use vehicles in Florida

Answer = B

Chapter Three: Defensive Driving

1) **In a double carriageway, if you need to turn right, where should you position your vehicle?**

   A. In the middle lane

   B. In the far left lane

   C. In the far right lane

   D. at the shoulder

Answer = C

2) **A school bus stopped the bus stop with a flashing red light, and the left arm stretched. What should you do?**

   A. Slow down and pass with care

   B. Be sure the school children are not alighting from the bus before moving

   C. Stop about ten feet from the bus

D. Pass with you horn sounding

Answer = C

3) **You are emerging into a freeway from the freeway ramp. What should you do before joining the traffic?*****
   A. Flag down vehicles on the freeway before joining
   B. Use your turning light and join the road while the vehicles on the freeway slow down for you
   C. Make use of your side mirror and turn to look over your shoulder
   D. Join the road immediately while activating your hazard light and headlight

Answer = C

4) **You are joining the freeway from a ramp. You should:**
   A. Join as soon as you emerge
   B. Increase your speed before joining

C. Attain the freeway speed limit before entering

D. Accelerate to the speed of the crossing freeway traffic

Answer = D

5) **What should be the following distance for a car following a motorcycle?*****
   A. Length of the car
   B. Two seconds following distance
   C. Three seconds following distance
   D. Four seconds following distance

Answer = D

6) **When a pedestrian is crossing the road, and a driver is turning, who must yield for the other?**
   A. The driver
   B. The pedestrian
   C. The faster road user
   D. The slower road user

Answer = A

7) **Which of the following should you do when approaching a bend?**

   A. Sound your hour

   B. Indicate the side of bend you will be turning

   C. Apply your brake pedals as soon as you get to the bend

   D. Before getting to a curve, always slow down

Answer = D

8) **Smaller vehicles have bigger blindspot than large vehicles.**

   A. True

   B. False

Answer = B

9) **While driving along a street, a ball sudden rolled out between the cars in front. What should you do?**

   A. Slow down gently, and be on the lookout for children and be ready to stop

B. Stop your vehicle and signal the children to fetch the ball

C. Maintain your speed but make sure you sound your horn to prevent anyone from crossing

D. Maintain your speed but make sure your headlight is constantly flashing

Answer = A

10) **You tried to back out from a parked position, what should you do if it seems difficult or children are playing around the area?**

a) Brighten the rear with the reverse light

b) Put your head through the window for clearer vision

c) Check the back of the care to confirm it is safe

d) Use the inner rear mirror

Answer = C

11) **A motorcycle is in your front. Always allow the motorcycle to have:**
    A. Half-width of the road
    B. Full width of the road
    C. The width of the motorcycle and half feet both direction
    D. Shared width with your vehicle

Answer = B

12) **Providing adequate stopping distance:**
    A. Leads to accident
    B. Reduce reaction time
    C. Allows for more time of reaction
    D. Leads to delay

Answer = C

13) **A truck is trying to pass you. You should:**
    A. Increase your speed
    B. Maintain the same pace with the truck
    C. Change your lane
    D. Release your acceleration pedal

Answer = D

14) **You missed your intended exit route while driving on a freeway. You should:**
    A. Drive on to the next exit road
    B. Reverse using the last lane
    C. Make a U-turn
    D. Reverse using the hard shoulder

Answer = A

15) **You are permitted to pass a school bus with a flashing red light and stop arm extended:** ***
    A. If you are driving on the far left
    B. If you are driving on the opposite side of a divided highway
    C. If no student is on the bus
    D. If no student is attempting to cross

Answer = B

16) **You can make a U-turn in residential districts only if:**

A. The road is narrow

B. There are no vehicle around

C. It a one-way street

D. There is a U-turn sign

Answer = B

17) **All passenger must wear a seat belt or restraint except:**

A. The driver

B. The passenger at the front seat

C. The passenger at the rear seat and babies

D. None of the above

Answer = D

18) **You are turning left into a side road across a three-lane highway. What should you do?**

A. Cross by edging forward carefully and cross each lane at a time

B. Flash your headlight as you cross

C. Ensure all three lanes are visible and free before crossing

D. Wait until you are signaled to cross by the opposing driver

Answer = C

19) **A defensive driver is one who:**
   A. looks around for possible hazard
   B. Drive slowly on the road
   C. Is cautious of the cars ahead
   D. Does not want to be hit by a following vehicle

Answer = A

20) **At a roundabout, which of the following has the right of way?**
   A. The driver already in the roundabout
   B. The driver entering the roundabout on the left-hand lane
   C. The driver entering the roundabout on the left-hand lane
   D. The first driver to arrive at the roundabout

Answer = D

21) **What is the normal following distance for a car under normal conditions?**

   A. One car length
   B. Three seconds gap
   C. Four seconds gap
   D. 25 feet

Answer = B

22) **Which of the following will need the most stopping time?**

   A. Car
   B. Truck
   C. Motorcycle
   D. Minibus

Answer = B

23) **Which of the following situation can lead to a collision on the road?**

   A. Fast-moving vehicles on the same lane
   B. Slow-moving vehicles on the same lane
   C. Fast-moving vehicle on different lanes

D. Fast and slow-moving vehicles on the same lane

Answer = D

24) **Car crashes involving teenagers are most likely when:**
   A. They are driving alone
   B. They are driving with any of the parents
   C. When they are driving with a teenager
   D. When they are driving with adults

Answer = C

25) **Which of the following speed should you be driving when merging into a freeway?**
   A. 50 MPH
   B. About the same speed as the vehicles on the freeway
   C. 65MPH
   D. The speed limit for the freeway

Answer = B

26) **Which of the following has the right of way at an intersection?**

A. No one

B. The driver traveling straight

C. The driver turning left

D. The driver turning right

Answer = A

27) **You are exiting a highway, at what point should you slow down?**

A. When you enter the exit lane

B. When you sight the exit lane

C. Just before exiting

D. When you are on the lane before the exit lane

Answer = A

28) **Which of the following best illustrate what you could do to avoid sleeping off while driving?**

a) Look for a place to rest on your journey

b) Provide enough water to drink on the way

c) Have people on the journey with you

d) Play non-soft music

Answer = A

29) **There is no law for the right of way at a four intersection but a vehicle at the intersection:**

   A. The driver going straight must yield to the one turning left

   B. The vehicle turning left must yield to the one going straight

   C. There is no law to who will yield

   D. The vehicle on the right will yield to the vehicle on the left

Answer = B

30) **A rule in defensive driving requires the driver to:**

   A. Maintain focus

B. Be confident and be attentive to what is happening

C. Always be at alert for possible hazard and keep the eyes moving

D. always look ahead for potential risk ahead on the road

Answer = C

31) **You observe the driver on a higher using a handheld phone. You should:**

A. Immediately alert the traffic police

B. Call 911

C. Increase your following distance

D. Signal the driver to stop the call

Answer = C

32) **You came across a herder with his animal. What should you do?**

A. Sound your horn to make them move away

B. Flash your light to alert the herder

C. Follow the instruction of the herder

D. Drive closer to the animal and proceed with care

Answer = C

33) You are on a freeway, driving on the far right lane. You should:***
A. Expect vehicles to merge on-ramp
B. Drive faster than the vehicles on the other lanes
C. Know that merging vehicle has the right of way
D. Honk as you pass every junction

Answer = A

34) You are about entering a freeway. You must:
A. Honk as you merge***
B. Use your inside and outside mirrors
C. Use all mirrors and turn your ahead
D. Use your four emergency light

Answer = C

35) **In which of the following location will large trucks most likely to lose speed**

A. When approaching a hump
B. While going up a long and steep hill
C. While going down a long gradual hill
D. While making a turn on a long gradual curve

Answer = B

Chapter Four: Intersections and Turnings

1) **You are following a truck on a two-lane road. If the truck is turning right while you are on the left-hand lane, what should you do?*****

   A. Move to the right lane because the truck will be moving to the left

   B. Be prepared to stop because the truck will occupy part of the left lane

   C. Continue on your lane because the truck will continue on the right-hand lane

   D. Pass on the left-hand lane while sounding your horn

Answer = B

2) **Which of the following drivers have the right of way?**
   A. The driver already in traffic flow
   B. The driver entering the traffic flow
   C. The driver about to pull out from a parked position
   D. All of the above

Answer = A

3) **From what distance to a turning point should you start indicating your turning signal?**
   A. 25 feet
   B. 50 feet
   C. 75 feet
   D. 100 feet

Answer = D

4) **While waiting to make a left turn at an intersection, you should:**

A. Continuously sound your horn as you go through

B. Continuously flash your light as you go through so that the opposing vehicle can yield

C. Indicate your signal and wait for a gap to turn while your front wheels face straight

D. Turn your front wheels to the left as you signal

Answer = C

5) **At what point can you legally block an intersection?**

A. When there are fewer vehicles on the intersection

B. When the intersection has three lanes

C. When the traffic light is still green

D. No time

Answer = D

6) **You arrive at an intersection with a flashing red light. What should you do?**

A. Wait for the red light

B. Wait for the green light

C. Stop before proceeding

D. Continue without stopping

Answer = C

7) **You arrived at an intersection with neither a stop nor a yield sign. What should you do?**

A. Sound your horn to put other drivers at alert

B. Flash you headlight to caution the other drivers before crossing

C. Release your acceleration pedal and be prepared to stop

D. Take the right-hand lane

Answer = C

8) **When you turn left into a one-way street from a two-way street, which side of the street should you position?**

   A. In the middle of the street

   B. In the left side of the street

   C. In the right side of the street

   D. On the parking lane

Answer = B

9) **When turning right to a right side street, which part of the street should you position?**

   A. In the middle of the street

   B. In the left side of the street

   C. In the right side of the street

   D. On the parking side of the street

Answer = C

10) **You parked your vehicle facing uphill of the road, where will your wheel be facing?**

    A. Forward

    B. Away from the street

C. Towards the street

D. None of the above

Answer = C

11) **You are following a driving whose left arm is extending upward. What does this signify?**

A. He is turning left

B. He is turning right

C. He is going straight

D. He is making a U-turn

Answer =B

12) **Why do you need enough gap to be available before joining an existing traffic flow?**

A. To speed up to the existing traffic speed

B. To allow other vehicles enough room to pass

C. To avoid the sounding of the horn

D. To slow the speed of the following vehicles

Answer = A

13) **You are joining an intersection from a minor road. What should you do?**

   A. Enter the intersection as soon as you emerge

   B. Give way to the traffic on the major road

   C. Pull in gradually until you fully join

   D. Flag down the traffic on the major road as you enter

Answer = B

14) **The green traffic light is beaming, if the intersection is still congested, what should you do?**

   A. Do not enter the intersection until the traffic clears

   B. Join the intersection and stay behind the traffic

   C. Join another lane in the intersection

   D. Surge forward until a gap is created for you

Answer = A

15) **You are at the intersection trying to cross when you noticed an emergency vehicle with a flashing light. What should you do?**

A. Pullover to the middle of the intersection

B. Use your emergency light

C. Stop at your position for the emergency vehicle to pass

D. Continue through the intersection before giving way

Answer = D

16) **If you hear a siren, you should pull to the side of the road immediately, even if you have not seen the vehicle.**

A. True

B. False

Answer = A

17) **You are following a driver whose left hand and arm are extended downward, what do you understand by that?**

A. The turning is turning left

B. The driver is turning right

C. The driving is planning to stop

D. The driver is going straight

Answer = C

18) **You need to turn right at an intersection of a two-way road into a two-way street, where should you position?**

A. On the far right-hand lane

B. On the far left-hand lane

C. In the middle of the lanes

D. On the road shoulder

Answer = A

19) **Two vehicles are at the intersection at the same time. Which should yield for the other?**

A. The one on the right should yield for the one one on the left

B. The one on the left should yield for the one on the right

C. None should yield

D. None has the right of way

Answer = B

20) **When two drivers arrive at an intersection from the opposite direction at the same time, the driver turning left must yield for the driver going straight or turning right.** ***

A. True

B. False

Answer = A

21) **The light is green at an intersection, but the straight moving vehicles from the opposite direction are still crossing. If you are turning left, what should you do?**

A. Wait at the pedestrian crossing

B. Enter and wait at the intersection for the straight moving vehicles

C. Enter the intersection and proceed to the next junction or left turn.

D. All of the above

Answer = B

22) **You are driving on a three-lane road and need to make a lane change to the right. What should you do?**

A. Look through your left side mirror

B. Look through both your left side and right side mirrors

C. Check the rearview and right side mirror before looking over your shoulder

D. Look over your shoulder

Answer = C

23) **At which speed do you complete your turn at an intersection?**

A. At a reduced speed than you used to enter

B. At a faster speed than you used to enter

C. At the speed limit of the road

D. At the speed at which you entered the intersection

Answer = D

24) You are making a turn. Which of the following should you do while turning?

A. Not change your gear

B. Not have the brake pushed down

C. Not have the clutch pedal pushed down

D. all of the above

Answer = D

25) You need to make a left turn. You should:

A. Make a half turn

B. Make a turn to the left and gradually enter the opposing lane

C. Stop in your lane with your wheel not turned until the road is clear

D. Flash your headlight on the oncoming vehicle as a signal for them to yield

Answer = D

26) **You are on the red light at an intersection, but you need to turn right. What should you do?**
   A. Wait for the green light
   B. Make the turn as the red light is not for you
   C. Unless a sign forbids, stop completely and ensure the road is clear before turning
   D. You are on your right so, proceed

Answer = C

27) **You are permitted to make a U-turns in which of the following situations?**
   A. If vehicles in both directions can see you 500 feet from afar
   B. If you take your correct position before arriving at the junction
   C. When you are on a multilane road

D. If there is a traffic light in place

Answer = A

28) **Which of the following is correct?**

A. You cannot make a U-turn at a traffic controlled intersections

B. It is not permitted to make a U-turn at an intersection not too far from a curve

C. Near a crest or hill, you are not permitted to make a U-turns

D. All of the above

Answer = D

29) **Which of the following is correct about U-turn?**

A. It is a safe driving procedure

B. It is hazardous

C. It is easy to perform

D. It can interfere with other traffic

Answer = B

30) You need to change to another lane. Without looking over your shoulder, you gradually joined the lane while looking at the side mirror in the direction of your turn. This method helps to eliminate blind spots.

A. True

B. False

Answer = B

31) The light at the intersection has turn green. What should you do next?

A. Yield to pedestrians at the intersection

B. Wait for vehicles, bicycle, motorcycle or pedestrians at the intersection

C. Wait three seconds before moving

D. Wait for four seconds before moving

Answer = B

32) You are turning after the intersection. What should you do?

A. Use your hazard light

B. Use your turn signal before the intersection

C. Use your turn signal after you pass the intersection

D. Use your turn signal when you are at the middle of the intersection

Answer = C

33) **You arrived at an intersection that the traffic light is not functioning. What should you do?**

A. Stop and proceed if safe

B. Be patient and allow other vehicles to pass

C. Drive to the intersection and continue without stopping

D. Slow down and drive pass without stopping

Answer = A

34) **If a driver cannot see traffic at all sides of an intersection, before getting to the intersection, he should be driving at:**

A. 15 mph

B. 20 mph

C. 25 mph

D. 30 mph

Answer = A

35) **You are at a controlled intersection, waiting to turn right. A pedestrian is waiting to cross the street you are to enter. If the traffic light turns green, which of you has the right of way?**

A. You have the right of way because the light has turned green

B. You have the right of way because there is no dedicated crosswalk there

C. The pedestrian has the right of way

D. Whoever arrives the junction first has the right of way

Answer = C

Chapter Five: Driving Conditions

1) **It has been raining for a few minutes, and the road condition is slippery. If you need to stop, what should you do?**

   A. Apply the brake gently and steadily

   B. Apply the brake sharply

   C. Pump the brake to stop

   D. Remove your leg from the accelerating pedal

Answer = A

2) **You are driving on the expressway and ready to take the next turn on your right. When will you use your right signal?**

   A. As soon as you see the turning point

   B. 100 feet before your turning point

   C. When you are three cars to the turning point

D. Just before you begin to turn

Answer = B

3) **The road becomes more slippery:*****
    A. After a heavy downpour
    B. A long period after starting
    C. Few minutes into the rain
    D. All of the above

Answer = C

4) **It has been dried for two months before a sudden drizzle. Which condition should you be careful of while driving?**
    A. Evaporation
    B. Slippery surface
    C. Dirty surface
    D. Muddy surface

Answer = B

5) **You are driving in foggy weather. Which of the following light is most appropriate for use?**

   A. High beam

   B. Low beam

   C. Emergency light

   D. Inner light and brake light

Answer = B

6) **You have just drifted off the road and now in the soft shoulder of the road. You should ease the gas pedal and brake gently. When the car has slowed down, ensure there is no traffic behind before steering gently onto the road pavement?**

   A. True

   B. False

Answer = A

7) **The fog is dense, and visibility has reduced. Which of the following light should you use?**

A. Headlight full beam

B. Headlight low beam

C. Flashing headlight

D. Flashing hazard light

Answer = B

8) **The sign below means**

A. Gravel road ahead

B. Slippery surface ahead

C. Snowy surface ahead

D. Curvy road ahead

Answer = B

9) **Which of the following conditions increases the freezing of the road?**

A. Curved road

B. Shade

C. Hill

D. Flat

Answer = B

10) **Driving in an expressway is not the same as driving in the street because:**

A. Expressway is easier to maneuver

B. Express has more and better lanes

C. Expressway requires fast thinking and better vehicle handling

D. The street is busier and involves a lot of attention and carefulness

Answer = C

11) **You are following a vehicle crossing a rail track. How should you follow?**

A. Allow the vehicle to finish crossing before you proceed

B. Follow behind immediately

C. Drive on the other lane of the road

D. Wait on the rail track while the front vehicle completes its passage

Answer = A

12) **You are driving on a rainy day, and the road maximum speed limit is 60 mph. Which of the following is most appropriate?**

A. Adhere to the stipulated speed limit on the road

B. Maintain the speed of the vehicle in your front

C. Ensure that you do not exceed the permitted speed limit

D. Adjust your speed limit to the road condition

Answer = D

13) **It is best practice to maintain the speed limit of the road when making a bend?**

A. True

B. False

Answer = B

14) **Which of the following is the effect of braking firmly when going through a curve?**

A. Skidding

B. Slip

C. Screech

D. None of the above

Answer = A

15) **Which of the following can lead to a collision on the road?*****

A. Following the maximum speed limit of the way

B. Adjusting your speed limit to the road condition

C. Driving on the far left lane

D. Driving faster or slower than other vehicles on the road

Answer = D

16) **Which of the following is most likely not to lead to collisions?**
   A. Driving slower than other vehicles
   B. Braking suddenly
   C. Effective speed adjustment
   D. Making sudden stops and turns

Answer = C

17) **You were driving on the fast lane and observed that a car wants to pass you by your right side, what should you do?**
   A. Increase your speed
   B. Find a way to move to the right if it is safe to do so
   C. Signal the car driver to pass on the right-hand side
   D. Do not allow the car to pass

Answer = B

18) You are driving on the far left lane on a three-lane road. You looked through the internal rearview mirror and observed that there are about five vehicles behind you. What should you do?

A. Give way by pulling to the right-hand lane

B. Continue with your driving on the same lane

C. Turn on your emergency light

D. All of the above

Answer = A

19) It has rained, and you are driving beyond 45 mph. Your steering feels very light, and it is like you are riding on top of the water. This phenomenon is known as:

A. Cruising

B. Strolling

C. Slipping

D. Hydroplaning

Answer = D

20) **You feel your vehicle is hydroplaning. What should you do?*****

A. Apply your brake immediately

B. Pull over and check your tires

C. Release your acceleration pedal

D. Increase your speed a little if it is safe to do so

Answer = C

21) **You are driving at night. The headlight of the oncoming vehicle is on full beam. The beam affects your ability to see the road. What should you do?*****

A. Use your full beam to counter the other beam

B. Release the acceleration pedal and focus on the right edge of the road

C. Gaze directly onto the headlight of the oncoming vehicle to reduce the effect

D. Shut your eyes temporarily until you pass the oncoming vehicle

Answer = B

22) **You saw a single headlight beam coming toward you while driving at night. You should:*****
   A. Maintain your position so long you are in your right of way
   B. Drive as fast as possible to pass the light
   C. Move as far to the right as possible
   D. Allow a width for a possible motorcycle passage

Answer = C

23) **Which of the following road users is the easiest to see at night?**
   A. Pedestrian
   B. Motorbike
   C. Car
   D. Bicycle

Answer = C

24) **Which of the following is a reason for not driving when there is a flood?**
   A. Road collapse
   B. Vehicles could be swept away
   C. Debris floating and other hazardous condition in the water
   D. All of the above

Answer = D

25) **It has not rained for a very long time. When you observe rain for the first time, what should you do?*****
   A. Reduce your speed due to possible slippery surface
   B. Try to get back home as fast as possible
   C. Prepare to use your brake more often
   D. Prepare to use your hazard light

Answer = A

26) The weather is bad. Therefore, visibility has reduced to less than 100 feet. What speed should you be driving?

A. 10 mph

B. 25 mph

C. 35 mph

D. 40 mph

Answer = C

27) Which of the following is the best material to carry in a snowy condition?

A. Some bottles of warm water

B. Anti-freeze pump

C. Extra tire

D. Wheel chain

Answer = D

28) You have finished crossing a flooded area. What should be the best action for you to take?***

A. Drive a bit faster to remove any debris underneath the car

B. Pull over and remove the mud on the body of the car

C. Use the wiper fluid and the wipe to clean the windscreen

D. Check your brake to be sure they are functioning fine

Answer = D

29) **You are going on a casual visit to a friend's place, which you have scheduled, and appointment. The journey will take about two hours. The weather is terrible, but you have prepared for the trip. Which of the following options would you consider best?**

A. Drive with care while on the journey

B. Call your friend and postpone the trip

C. Make sure you have your wheel chain

D. Ensure your car does not overheat

Answer = B

30) You need to check that the pressure of your tire is within the recommended range. Where in the vehicle will you find pressure indicator in pound per square inch (PSI)?

A. On the side window
B. On the dashboard close to the driver
C. In the inside edge of the vehicle door
D. On the lower right corner of the front windshield

Answer = C

31) You observed that your vehicle is losing traction while driving after a rainfall. You should:***

A. Be firm and maintain your speed
B. Carefully increase your speed a little
C. Slow down by removing your leg from the accelerating pedal
D. Maintain firm grip of the steering and apply the brake gently

Answer = C

32) **Due to weather conditions, you had to use your windshield wiper. Which of the following do you have to use too?*****

A. Headlight

B. Hazard light

C. Inner light

D. Honk your horn

Answer = A

33) **You are told by a traffic officer to continue with your driving at an intersection with the red light. You should:*****

A. Wait for the green light to come on first

B. Obey the traffic officer's instruction

C. Slow down and stop

D. Stop before obeying the traffic officer's instruction

Answer = B

34) **The road is slippery. What should you do?**

A. Pay attention to the vehicle behind you

B. Use your brake often

C. Always apply your brake firmly

D. Do not make a fast turn

Answer = D

35) **The rain has stopped, and you are driving on a roadway. You should:**

A. Apply the two seconds following rule

B. Increase the gap between your vehicle and the vehicle in front

C. Apply the three seconds following

D. Give three feet when passing

Answer = B

Chapter Six: Passing

1) **You are driving on an expressway with three-lane. A car attempts to overtake you by the right. What does this tell you, and what action would you take?**
   A. The road has narrowed down, so you need to speed up
   B. You are driving slowly and need to move to the right lane
   C. You are driving too slow and need to speed up
   D. You are in order, so continue as per your present situation

Answer = B

2) **If a car you once saw behind you begins to pass, what should you do?*****

A. Speed up to avoid a collision

B. Slow down a bit

C. Maintain the speed of the passing vehicle

D. Change your lane immediately

Answer = B

3) **You need to overtake the vehicle in front of you. When can you do that?**

   A. When the single yellow line separating the road is solid

   B. When there is a double solid yellow line demarcating the road

   C. When the double yellow line on your side of the road is solid

   D. When there is a broken yellow line on your side of the road

Answer = D

4) **Which of the following action of a passing vehicle is not wrong?**

A. Passing by the right because there is no sign against it

B. Passing by the right when it is safe to do so

C. Indicating your side of passing on time before proceeding

D. None of the above

Answer= D

5) **You were about to pass a vehicle in front of you. If the vehicle finally slows down and stops before a crosswalk, what should you do?**

A. Use the opportunity and pass

B. Blow your horn and pass

C. Slow down and pass carefully

D. Slow down and stop

Answer = D

6) **Which of the following is not necessary before passing the vehicle in your front?**

A. Looking over your shoulder

B. Signaling of your lane change

C. Sounding your horn

D. Checking in your mirrors

Answer = C

7) **You are driving on a two-lane single carriageway. If a school bus with a flashing red light stopped in the opposite lane, what should you do? *****

A. Stop completely for the red flashing light

B. Drive on since the bus is on the opposite lane

C. Slow down and be ready to stop

D. Slow down and proceed gradually

Answer = A

8) **You have passed a vehicle by the left and need to return to the right. What should you do before moving to the right?*****

A. Indicate your turn signal

B. Look through your rearview mirror

C. Ensure to see the front bumper of the passed vehicle

D. All of the above

Answer = D

9) **You need to pass the vehicle in front of you. What should you have in mind before passing?*****

   A. Though you have signaled, the front vehicle might not make way for you pass

   B. The vehicle might not slow down for you to finish your passing

   C. The front vehicle might not give you the space to return to the right after passing

   D. All of the above

Answer = D

10) **In which of the following situation should you pass a vehicle by the right on a two-lane road?*****

    A. When it parked by the curb

B. When turning to a right side road

C. When waiting to turn left

D. When parking to drop a passenger

Answer = C

11) **You were passing a bicycle when you sighted an oncoming car coming towards you. What should you do?*****

A. Speed up and pass the bicycle

B. Release your acceleration pedal to give way for the oncoming vehicle

C. Move closer to the bicycle to make room for the oncoming car

D. Sound your horn for the bicycle to give way

Answer = B

12) **You need to pass a vehicle in front. If there is a junction ahead, you should:**

A. Do the passing as quickly as possible

B. Do not pass until after the junction

C. Pass up to the front driver and request him to slow down

D. Sound your horn to let him give you space to pull back in

Answer = B

13) **You want to pass a long truck. You could see about 80 feet ahead fairly. You should:**

A. Sound your horn as you pass

B. Use your full headlight beam as you pass

C. Do not pass until you are sure of the road ahead

D. Speed up quickly and sound your horn as you pass

Answer = C

14) **It is safe to pass within 110 feet of a tunnel, intersection, bridge, rail crossing, or hill.**

A. True

B. False

Answer = B

15) **The vehicle in front is driving in the middle of a double lane road, making overtaking difficult. What should you do?**

   A. Follow the vehicle until there is enough space by the left to pass

   B. Pass through the available area using the shoulder

   C. Find a way through the left-hand side of the vehicle

   D. Sound your horn for the driver to give way

Answer = A

16) **In which of the following cases could you pass by the right-hand side of the vehicle in front?*****

   A. On a one-way street

   B. When the driver ahead is turning left

   C. When your direction of travel in an open highway is marked for two or more lanes

   D. All of the above

Answer = D

17) You are following a long vehicle. You are permitted to slightly tap your horn or flash your headlight before you pass

A. True

B. False

Answer = A

18) A truck flashed its headlight to alert you of its intention to pass on a two-lane road in your direction. You should:

A. Do not allow a bigger vehicle to pass you on a two-lane road

B. Speed up to create more space behind

C. Move to the right to give way

D. Signal to the left for the truck to go through your right-hand side

Answer = C

19) You are behind a vehicle traveling in your direction. You intend to pass the vehicle, but it is positioned on the left-hand side of

the two-lane road. If the road is a one-way
road, what should you do?

A. Follow behind until there is a space on the
right-hand side
B. Sound your horn for the driver to move to
the right
C. Pass using the right-hand lane
D. All of the above

Answer = C

20) **In which of the following situation are you
to return to your lane after passing another
vehicle?*****

A. After signaling to return to your lane
B. When you can see the driver from your
inside rear-view mirror
C. When you can see the headlight from the
inside rear-view mirror
D. After signaling and flagging down the
vehicle that you have passed

Answer = C

Chapter Seven: Traffic Control and Parking

1) **What is the meaning of a white and red sign often at an intersection?**

   A. The traffic light

   B. Always stop at the intersection

   C. Always look in both direction before crossing the intersection

   D. Slow down and be ready to stop if need be

Answer = D

2) **You are driving within a school area. The school crossing guard is on duty. What should you do?**

   A. Obey every traffic instruction of the guard

   B. Obey standard traffic rule and ignore the guard

C. The guard is not a traffic officer, so his directions are not for the public

D. Obey the guard's instruction when children are crossing

Answer = A

3) **The road sign in the shape of a rectangle denotes:**
   A. Warning sign
   B. Emergency sign
   C. Railway crossing
   D. Speed limit

Answer = D

4) **You parked by the side of the road to receive a call. You should:*****
   A. Keep your headlight on
   B. Keep your four-way flasher on
   C. Keep your inner light on
   D. Switch off the whole light

Answer = B

5) At a controlled intersection, you should obey.............. over the other***

A. Traffic light

B. Traffic sign

C. Police officer

D. Traffic markings

Answer = C

6) **Road sign in the shape of a diamond denotes which of the following:**

A. Traffic direction

B. Hazard ahead

C. Direction of traffic

D. Information on the weather

Answer = B

7) **When would you not cross a single broken white line or a broken yellow line?**

A. When turning to join a driveway

B. When doing so would affect the traffic flow

C. When passing a broken down vehicle

D. None of the above

Answer = B

8) **In which of the following situation would you increase the distance between you and the vehicle in your front? *****
   A. When another vehicle is tailgating you
   B. When the vehicle beside you is making a right turn
   C. When you are driving at a speed slower than the posted maximum speed limit
   D. When there is a wide gap between you and the vehicle behind

Answer = A

9) **There are two sets of solid yellow lines separated by two feet or more: *****

A. They can be crossed when you need to pass a slow vehicle by the left

B. Can be used when making a left turn

C. Can be crossed only my motorcycles

D. They are like a solid wall that should not be crossed

Answer = D

10) **You are to turn right at a junction, but the traffic light is on red. If pedestrians are crossing, and a sign below is posted. You should:*****

A. Give way to the pedestrians before you continue

B. Continue carefully for the pedestrians to give way

C. You are not to continue until the light turns green

D. You are to cross only when all hazards have been cleared

Answer = C

11) **Why should a driver that passed a flashing red traffic light not be fined?**

A. He crossed without stopping

B. He was crossing after slowing down

C. He stopped before crossing

D. He sounded the horn before crossing

Answer = C

12) **You saw a yellow traffic light at an intersection. What should you do?**

A. Prepare to stop at the intersection

B. Cross when you get to the intersection

C. Prepare to drive by the right lane

D. Slow down and cross carefully

Answer = A

13) **You are driving on the road with a broken yellow line and a solid yellow line about a foot from each apart. What do the lines indicate?*****

A. Either of the vehicles should cross the lines

B. Only the vehicle on the side of the solid yellow line could cross the lines

C. Under no circumstance should the lines be crossed

D. Only the vehicle on the side of the broken yellow line could cross the lines

Answer = D

14) **You are to turn right at a junction, but the traffic light is on red. If pedestrians are crossing, you should:*****

A. Give way to the pedestrians before you continue

B. Continue carefully for the pedestrians to give way

C. You are not to continue until the light turns green

D. You are not to cross even when all hazards have been cleared

Answer = A

15) **You are at an intersection with a flashing amber light pointing left. If you intend to turn left, what would you do? *****
   A. Continue with the left
   B. Continue after yielding to other road users
   C. Wait for the light to turn green
   D. Wait for the light to stop flashing

Answer = B

16) **You are turning left at an intersection. If the traffic light has turned green, but there are vehicles within the intersection. What should you do?*****
   A. You have the right of way, so you are clear to proceed
   B. Occupy the available space within the intersection

C. Wait for the intersection to clear before you enter

D. Enter the intersection and use the right-hand lane

Answer = C

17) **What is the function of the parallel yellow lines in the middle of the road that is used by two-way traffic traveling in the opposite direction?**

A. To separate vehicles moving in the opposite direction

B. To direct vehicle traveling on a highway

C. To separate vehicles moving in the same direction

D. To mark the none entry side of the road

Answer = A

18) **In which of the following situations would you not cross a solid yellow line?**

A. When you are instructed at a construction zone

B. When you need to turn left to enter a driveway or premises

C. When you need to pass a slow-moving vehicle

D. When a sign instructs you to do so due to the work zone ahead

Answer = C

19) **You are traveling on a three-lane highway. If you are driving on the far left lane, which lane number would you be?*****

A. 1

B. 2

C. 3

D. None of the above

Answer = A

20) You arrived at an intersection that has a crosswalk before it, a stop sign, but without a stop line. You should stop:

A. On the crosswalk

B. Before you reach the crosswalk

C. After the crosswalk

D. Before the intersection

Answer = B

21) If you are driving on a two-lane roadway in your direction, which of the lanes will be considered the smoothest driving lane?

A. The left lane

B. The right lane

C. Both lanes

D. None of the lanes

Answer = B

22) Two solid double yellow lines are about two feet apart. While driving along these solid lines, you should: ***

A. Cross to the left only when you need to enter a driveway
B. Drive on the line as long as you do not cross it
C. Cross only when you need to make a U-turn
D. Consider it a barrier and never cross or drive on it

Answer = D

23) **You are on a two-lane road in the same direction. If the lane within your position is marked with a double solid white line, what does it imply?**

A. You can cross the line to pass the vehicle in front by the left only

B. You can cross line the pass the vehicle in front by the right only

C. Wait for the broken single white line before changing lane

D. You can change lane when required

Answer = C

24) What is the meaning of the sign below?

A. A hill ahead

B. There is a low zone ahead

C. There is a crest ahead

D. There is a detour ahead

Answer = B

25) **If you come across this sign, what should you do?*****

A. Slow down a drive with care

B. Slow down and be ready to yield for any traffic or pedestrian

C. Slow down and stop completely then yield for any traffic or pedestrian

D. Slow down and but be careful of traffic as you have the right of way

Answer = B

26) **What does this sign signify?**

A. A narrow roadway ahead

B. A two-way street ahead

C. A divided road ends ahead

D. Traffic merging ahead

Answer = D

27) You come across this sign. What should you **do?**

A. This is a "shark teeth" you are free to proceed

B. You can cross the intersection at the approved speed limit of the road

C. Slow down and yield if there is a pedestrian or motorists crossing

D. Stop completely before the triangular "shark teeth" sign and wait for any pedestrian or motorist tending to cross

Answer = C

28) What does this sign indicate?

A. Pass on either side of the island

B. Overtake on either side

C. Enter by the right and exit by the left

D. A single lane ahead

Answer = A

29) **Pedestrians are crossing an unmarked crosswalk. When you drive to such a location, what should you do?**

A. Yield to the crossing pedestrian

B. Sound your horn to alert them of your presence

C. Slow down and continue with your trip

D. You have the right of way, so proceed with your trip

Answer = A

30) You came across this sign as you move around town. This sign indicates that you are around:

A. A court zone

B. A pedestrian crossing area

C. A library

D. A school zone

Answer = D

31) You were driving around town in a new city. If you see this sign, what does it tell you?***

A. You need to move to the next

B. You are driving against traffic

C. You are heading to a dangerous zone

D. The lane leads to nowhere

Answer = B

32) **You saw this sign while on the highway. What does it indicate?**

A. An island divided road ahead

B. A traffic control lane ahead

C. The end of a divided highway

D. Double curved road ahead

Answer = C

33) **You arrived at a parking lot with different markings. The marking for persons with disability is in:*****

A. White

B. Blue

C. Red

D. Yellow

Answer = B

34) **A couple went for groceries shopping. If the place they parked along the road has a yellow mark on the curb, what should they do?**

A. One person should go into the grocery store while the other stay in the car

B. Both should go into the store together with the car locked and secured

C. The parking area is restricted for those with disability

D. Parking within the yellow-painted curb is illegal

Answer = A

35) There is a length of red-painted curbs with the word "BUSES" written on it. This means that:

A. Buses are not permitted to park within the red area

B. Only buses are permitted to park within the red area

C. Cars are permitted to park within the area marked red

D. No vehicle is to park within the red area

Answer = B

36) You parked along a length of green painted curbs as you go for shopping. What should you do when you get down from the car?

A. Hurry into the groceries store

B. Secure your vehicle

C. Look for the permitted parking time limit

D. Pay for the parking before proceeding with the shopping

Answer = C

37) **There are special plates for drivers with disabilities. If you have to pick up a person with a disability with your car and you parked at the space for the disabled, and a law enforcement officer accosts you, you should:**

A. Inform the officer you are picking up a disable

B. Sure the officer your plate number

C. Request the office to give you time for the person with a disability to come out of the place

D. Show the officer your placard

Answer = D

38) **While searching for a place to park, you avoided the disabled person's parking space**

and parked adjacent to it on a crosshatched diagonal line area. You have:***

A. Parked in a no-parking zone

B. Parked on private parking space

C. Parked in a free zone

D. Parked correctly

Answer = A

39) A person with a disability has been found guilty of interchanging the placard with a family or friend. He could be:

A. Fined $1000, up to 6 months imprisonment or both

B. Imprisoned for a month or have the driver's license revoked

C. Fine $500, or imprisonment for up to 6 months

D. Relieved of his rights and villages as a person living with a disability for 6 months

Answer = A

40) **The placard or plate of a deceased, disabled person has to be:**

A. Destroy

B. Returned to DMV

C. Inform the DMV

D. Kept out of use of others

Answer = B

41) **What does this sign mean?**

A. Parking area

B. No parking

C. Park within the indicated range

D. Parking allowed within a specific time

Answer = B

42) **Which of the following does not constitute illegal parking?*****

A. Parking within 14 feet of a fire hydrant

B. Parking between a safety zone and a curb

C. Parking on a freeway

D. Parking by a curb colored white

Answer = D

43) Which of the following options is correct?

A. You may leave the engine of your vehicle running if you are leaving it for a short time

B. If you must park by a curb on a street that is leveled, do so with the front wheel pointing the curb

C. You are allowed only a short period of interference of vehicle with the door when alighting from a car

D. Disable person with a placard can park on a restricted zone as long as they obey the permitted length of parking

Answer = D

44) **Which of the following is correct about parking on a freeway?**

A. You must park away from the pavement

B. You must stay in your vehicle with the locked until help arrives

C. You must provide adequate space for passing vehicles

D. All of the above

Answer = D

45) **If you park along the freeway, your vehicle should be:**

A. Visible to other vehicles in both direction for at least 200 feet

B. Seen by other vehicles in both directions for at least 150 feet

C. Visible to other vehicles at least 100 feet in both direction

D. At least 150 feet visible on the near lane and 100 feet visible on the far lane

Answer = A

Chapter Eight: Emergency

1) **Which of the following reduces the effect of fatal accidents on the road**
   A. Driving at night
   B. Driving when it is sunrise and sunset
   C. Avoid driving during rush hour
   D. Make proper use of the seat belts

Answer = D

2) **There is an oncoming car on the other lane, and a cyclist is riding in your front. What should you do?*****
   A. Pass the cyclist and the car at the middle
   B. Increase your speed to pass the cyclist
   C. Reduce your speed for the car to pass first
   D. Sound your horn for the cyclist to move further right

Answer = C

3) Which of the following driving surface can cause a vehicle to skid?

A. Gravel road
B. Icy road
C. Dried asphalt surface
D. Dusty road

Answer = B

4) You are driving to work through a curvy route on a wet Monday morning. If the maximum speed limit for the road is 60 mph, which speed limit could be most appropriate for you?***

A. 25 mph
B. 65 mph
C. 60 mph
D. 50 mph

Answer = A

5) **What should be the following distance when following a motorcycle?*****

    A. Two-second following distance

    B. Three-second following distance

    C. Four-second following distance

    D. Five seconds following distance

Answer = C

6) **An emergency vehicle is some feet behind you. You should:*****

    A. Stop immediately

    B. Reduce your speed for the vehicle to pass

    C. Drive to the edge of the road and pull up

    D. Drive to the edge of the road and continue at a very reduce speed for the vehicle to pass

Answer = C

7) **You should always look ahead to check for possible hazards before you arrive there. If you are driving at night and another vehicle**

beams its full headlight on you, what should you do?***

A. Look ahead and focus on the tire of the oncoming vehicle

B. Look ahead and focus on your vision behind the beam of the headlight

C. Look ahead with your focus on the right edge of your lane

D. Focus your attention on the left-hand headlight

Answer = C

8) **You are involved in a significant collision with another vehicle. How long is required for you to make a report to the DMV?** ***

A. Within five days

B. Within ten days

C. Within two weeks

D. Within twenty days

9) **You were driving on a wet road when you observed your car skidding. You should:**

A. Use your hand brake

B. Apply your brake

C. Press your leg on the acceleration pedal

D. Turn the steering wheel to face the direction of the skid

Answer = D

10) **Your car begins to slip on a slippery surface. You should:**

   A. Hit the accelerator

   B. Pull up your hand brake

   C. Get a wheel on the dry shoulder of the road

   D. Turn on your four-side emergency light

Answer = C

11) **You applied your brake to stop your vehicle from skidding but was not successful. Which of the following would be a better option to stop the vehicle from continuing skidding on a snowy weather?**

   A. Gradually pedal down the brake

   B. Engage the car in neutral

C. Turn of the engine

D. Gradually edge into a snowbank

Answer = D

12) **On wet or snowy weather, which of the following is not a way of avoiding skidding?**

A. Giving enough gap between you and the vehicle in front

B. Driving slowly

C. Avoiding rapid stop

D. Turning the steering wheel quickly

Answer = D

13) **You have passed a flooded area and need to dry your brake. What should you do?**

A. Park the car for some minuted to dry

B. Slightly press the accelerator and the brake at the same time until the brake dries up

C. Rapidly step on the brake system after gaining speeding for a couple of time

D. Keep driving, and the brake will naturally dry

Answer = B

14) **You brake harshly while trying to stop. This causes the wheel of your vehicle to lock. Which of the following will you do to unlock the wheel?**
   A. Pedal your accelerator
   B. Release your brake
   C. Put the gear in neutral
   D. Engage your hand brake

Answer = B

15) **Which of the following helps to stop the locking of a vehicle?**
   A. Anti-lock brake system
   B. Anti-lock accelerating system
   C. Automated brake pad
   D. Automated accelerating system

Answer = A

16) **Which of the following should not be applied if the accelerator of a vehicle gets stuck?**

   A. Shift the gear to neutral

   B. Apply the brakes

   C. Use your right foot to raise the accelerating pedal

   D. Try to drive the car safely off the road

Answer = C

17) **Which of the following is not a cause of collision on the road?**

   A. Driving at an unsafe speed

   B. Making an improper turn

   C. The distraction of the driver

   D. Signaling about 100 feet before turning

Answer = D

18) **Which of the following should you do if you find a vehicle's hazard light ahead of you?**

A. Drive to another lane and pass quickly

B. Stop and assist if requested

C. Block the road to stop other vehicles to assist at the emergency

D. All of the above

Answer = B

19) **A driver got involved in a collision, and luckily he was not injured. If he does not know the condition of the other driver, what must he do first?**

A. Drive away from the scene immediately

B. Get the vehicle off the road

C. Confirm the condition of the other driver

D. Leave the vehicle on the road

Answer = C

20) **If a driver is involved in a collision that resorted to the death or injury to someone, the driver, his legal representative, or his insurance broker will prepare a report in**

writing to the DMV, not later than 10 days of the incident.

A. True

B. False

Answer = A

21) You collided with another vehicle, which caused other vehicles to stop because the road has been blocked by your vehicle and that of the other driver. If none of you were injured, what must you do next?

A. Get the vehicles off the road

B. Call 911

C. Leave the vehicles on the road

D. Request the other driver to repair your vehicle

Answer = A

22) After a collision, a driver discovers that a passenger has been injured. What should he do?

A. Drive the injured to the hospital

B. Call 911

C. Move your vehicle out of the road

D. Control other vehicles

Answer = B

23) **If you are involved in an accident, which of the following should you show to the other driver?*****

A. Driver's License and current address

B. Evidence of financial responsibilities

C. Vehicle registration card

D. All of the above

Answer = D

24) **If you get involved in a collision, you must make a report to DMV within:*****

A. 20 days

B. 15 days

C. 10 days

D. 5 days

Answer = C

25) **If you hit a parked car or a property, which of the following must you do?**

    A. Write your name and address on a paper and attach on the damaged car or property

    B. Leave a note with your phone number and attach to the property or car

    C. Report the incident to the DMV

    D. All of the above

Answer = D

26) **You hit an animal and got it injured. You should:**

    A. Driveaway

    B. Move the animal

    C. Call humane society or police

    D. Drag the animal to the corner and move on

Answer = C

27) **A road user was slightly injured when he got hit by your car. What should you do?**

A. Pay the person $1000

B. Report to DMV within 10 days

C. Report to DMV within 5 day

D. Take over the treatment of the person

Answer = B

28) **Which of the following is correct in case of an accident?*****

A. File a report with DMV with form MV-104

B. Inform the police to make a report of the accident

C. Inform the DMV as to make a report of the accident

D. Send a mail report to the DMV

Answer = A

29) **You have been involved in an accident but never reported. What could happen to you?**

A. Suspension of driving privilege

B. 4 years of jail term

C. 3 years of jail term

D. $5000 fine

Answer = A

30) **You were involved in an accident, but the other driver was found to be at fault. If your insurance was discovered not proper, what would the authority do?**
   A. You could be jail for four year
   B. You could be jailed for three years
   C. You could lose your driving privilege for two years
   D. You could lose your driving privilege for four years

Answer = D

31) **You suffered a breakdown and have called for assistance. What should you do next?**
   A. Stay behind your vehicle
   B. Stay in front of your vehicle
   C. Return to your vehicle and belt up
   D. Stay some few distances away from your car

Answer = C

32) **If you have a breakdown in a freeway without enough shoulder. What should you do if the shoulder is not enough to occupy the full width of your vehicle?**

A. Exit your vehicle and stay behind

B. Exit your vehicle with your hazard light at your discretion and move to a safe zone

C. Exit your vehicle and move to a safe zone, away from your vehicle

D. Stay in the car and belt up

Answer = B

33) **You arrived at an accident scene where the emergency service was already stationed and carrying out their operation, and traffic is under control. You should.**

A. Offer a gallon of gas and jump-starting of your vehicle

B. Assist with the control of traffic

C. Stop to assist the accident victims

D. Mind your driving

Answer = D

34) **If you get involved in a collision, it will be a traffic violation to leave the crash scene, and if it leads to a fatality, it becomes a criminal violation.**
  A. True
  B. False

Answer = D

35) **If your vehicle got stalled on a train track with the warning light flashing. What should you do?**
  A. Exit your vehicle and call the emergency Notification System
  B. Exit the vehicle and look for a tow van to tow the vehicle
  C. Exit the vehicle and call the railway station
  D. All of the above

Answer = A

Chapter Nine: Occupant Protection

1) **If you need to check the installation of your child's passenger restraint system, which agency would you contact?**

   A. The licensing office

   B. The local law enforcement agencies

   C. The fire departments

   D. A and B

Answer = D

2) **Which of the following actions would you consider most relevant as your child grows?**

   A. The child would not need the restraint system any longer

   B. Check the suitability of the restraint system

   C. Always clean the restraints system

D. The child can use the front seat

Answer = B

3) **Which of the following is correct?**

   A. Secure your child with a federally approved child passenger restrain

   B. Carry your child on the lap and secure with your hands

   C. Use a safety belt to secure your child depending on the age

   D. A and C

Answer = D

4) **A child is under two years old. How would the child be secured in a car?**

   A. Use a rear-facing child passenger restraint

   B. Use a federally approved seat belt

   C. Carry the child on your laps in the front seat

   D. Carry the child on your laps in the rear seat

Answer = A

5) **A child is seven years, eight months, and 4 feet 7 inches tall. What kind of restraint will the child require?**

    A. Cross shoulder belt

    B. Lap belt

    C. Child passenger restraint

    D. To be carried by an adult

Answer = C

6) In which of the following situation will an under 8 years old child be allowed to use an approved "child passenger restraint system" ride in the front seat of a vehicle?

    A. When the rear seat is not available in the vehicle

    B. If the proper installation of the restraint system in the rear-seat is not possible

    C. Due to medical reasons

    D. All of the above

Answer = D

7) You need to restrain your seven and a half years old child, but the rear seat has been occupied by a five-year-old, six-year-old, and six and a half years old children already restrained at the rear seat. What should you do?

A. Create a space at the rear seat

B. Get an adult to lap one of the kids at the rear seat to create a space

C. Restrain the seven and a half kid at the front seat using a proper seat restraint system

D. You can go without one of the children

Answer = C

8) How best would you restrain a child of 8 years old or older and 4 feet and 9 inches tall or higher?

A. Put the child in the back seat with a child passenger restraint system

B. Use a properly secured safety belt

C. Place the child between two adult passenger

D. Place the child between the rear door and an adult passenger

Answer = B

9) **A driver has an adult passenger and two children of ten years old and 8 years old. Who has the responsibility to ensure that the children are well secured in the vehicle?**

A. The driver

B. The adult passenger

C. The children

D. The law enforcement officer

Answer = A

10) **You are driving an airbag-equipped car. Which of the following positions should you not place a rear-facing passenger restraint system?**

A. In the front seat

B. In the middle of the rear seat

C. At the left side of the rear seat

D. At the right side of the rear seat

Answer = B

11) **An airbag protects the body if a collision occurs. What is the best position between the steering and the breastbone of the driver?**

   A. 8 inches

   B. 10 inches

   C. 15 inches

   D. 20 inches

Answer = B

12) **Which of the following is illegal?**

   A. Leaving a 12-year-old person unattended

   B. Leaving a child of 5 years 8 months old unattended in the car

   C. Leaving a child of 6 years old with a 13 years old person in the car

   D. All of the above

Answer = B

13) **Which of the following is not a cause of distraction on the road?**

    A. Having the mind off the road

    B. Having the eyes off the road

    C. Having the hands off the steering

    D. Having your leg of the accelerating pedal

Answer = D

14) **You receive a call while driving. What should you do?**

    A. Receive the call

    B. Put the call on speakout and receive it

    C. Use your hand free set

    D. Allow the phone ring to voice message

Answer = D

15) **You are visiting a friend in a different city. You are using the map as a guide. Which is the best way to check your route map as you go?**

    A. Intermittently view the map as you go

B. Check the map when you get to a traffic light

C. Pull up before checking the map

D. Confirm direction from a fellow driver

Answer = C

16) **You have an emergency, so you are expecting a call or a text message. If the text message arrives while driving, you should:**

A. Read the message

B. Reply to the message

C. Ignore the message

D. Call back instead.'

Answer = C

17) **Which of the following is not a distraction while driving?**

A. Listening to the news in the car

B. Putting a make call

C. Searching for things in the car

D. Reading

Answer = A

18) **Which of the following is correct?**
   A. Leaving your pet in a car with the windows fully up
   B. Leaving your pet in a car with your window slightly lowered
   C. Leaving a pet when the temperature is high
   D. None of the above

Answer = D

19) **The rear seat of your vehicle has a side airbag. What is the ideal distance from the side to the passenger sitting at the rear?**
   A. Not less than 10 inches
   B. 12 inches
   C. 15 inches
   D. 20 inches

Answer = A

20) Two adult passengers and a 12 years old passenger are at the rear-seat of your car. Who has the responsibility of making sure the 12 years old passenger is wearing a seat belt?

A. The passenger on the left

B. The driver

C. The passenger on the right

D. The 12 years old passenger

Answer = B

Chapter Ten: Road Laws and Rules

1) **A road user was injured during a collision. If the driver involved in the collision ran away, what could be his conviction?**

   A. One year

   B. Two years

   C. Three years

   D. Four years

Answer = A

2) **A road user was seriously injured when a driver was trying to evade the police. If the driver is convicted, he may be fined as much as:**

   A. $10,000

   B. $7,000

   C. $5,000

D. $2,000

Answer = D

3) **Which of the following traffic law is also taken as a drugged law?**
   A. Speed driving law
   B. Reckless driving law
   C. Drunk driving law
   D. Environmental hazardous driving law

Answer = C

4) **With a class C driver's license, a driver is allowed to tow up to .... Vehicles?**
   A. 1
   B. 2
   C. 3
   D. 4

Answer = A

5) You are convicted of leaving an accident scene in which no one was injured. You may receive a sentence of up to:

    A. Three months

    B. Six months

    C. Ten months

    D. One year

Answer = B

6) Which of the following persons will not be considered a pedestrian?

    A. A disable on a tricycle

    B. A disable using a car

    C. A disable on a wheelchair

    D. A disable on quadricycle

Answer = B

7) While driving along a street, you came across a pedestrian about crossing at an unmarked crosswalk. You should:

A. Stop for the pedestrian to cross before continuing

B. Proceed with your driving as you have the right of way

C. Sound your horn as a warning because the pedestrian is crossing at an illegal position

D. Follow up right behind the pedestrian

Answer = A

8) **You had an urgent call to attend to an emergency. You arrive at a crosswalk where two cars are waiting. What should you do?**

A. Wait behind the stopped cars

B. Sound your horn to alert the stopped cars

C. Use your emergency light

D. Look for available space and maneuver through

Answer = A

9) **You are close to a crosswalk when a pedestrian made eye contact with you. You should:**

   A. Continue driving

   B. Sound your horn and continue driving

   C. Stop for the pedestrian to cross the street

   D. Wave the pedestrian and continue driving

Answer = C

10) **When should you use your horn?*****

   A. When you are in an emergency

   B. While driving on a bust street

   C. When another driver makes a mistake

   D. If it will help to avoid a collision

Answer = D

11) **It is permitted to transport animals at the back of pickup truck when:*****

   A. The truck has a closed tailgate

   B. When the sideboard of the truck is up to 20 inches high

C. The animal is free to move around the back of the truck

D. The animal is properly secured

Answer = D

12) **There is a crosswalk ahead. What should you do?**

A. Maintain your speed and pass

B. Slow down and be prepared to stop before the stop line

C. Use your horn as you cross

D. Stop on the crosswalk as you see a pedestrian

Answer = B

13) **Where can you find crosswalk painted in yellow?**

A. At a crossing for hospital patients and visitors

B. At a road crossing in a market area

C. At a school crossing

D. All of the above

Answer = C

14) **A driver was passing a motorcyclist when he saw a pedestrian crossing the road. He slowed down in preparation to stop. Which of them has the right of way?**
   A. The pedestrian
   B. The driver
   C. The motorcyclist
   D. None of them

Answer = A

15) **You approach a crosswalk with a malfunctioning flashing yellow light. What should you do?**
   A. Stop
   B. Prepare to stop
   C. Drive on
   D. Sound your horn and proceed

Answer = B

16) **You arrived at an intersection before another vehicle. Who should yield to the other?**

   A. You yield for the other vehicle
   B. The other vehicle should yield to you
   C. Both of you can proceed at the same time
   D. The bigger vehicle should yield to the smaller vehicle

Answer = B

17) **You arrived at an intersection at the same time as another vehicle. If the vehicle tends to turn right, who has to yield?**

   A. You have to yield to the other vehicle
   B. The other vehicle should yield to you
   C. Both of you can proceed at the same time
   D. The bigger vehicle should yield to the smaller vehicle

Answer = A

18) **You are turning at a roundabout. The vehicle in your front is moving too slowly. You should:**

A. Pass the vehicle by the left side

B. Pass the vehicle by the right side

C. Honk for the vehicle to leave the road

D. Stay behind the vehicle until you branch off

Answer = D

19) **You slightly pass your exit route at a roundabout. What should you do?**

A. Pull up by the right-hand side and reverse

B. Pull up by the right-hand side and wait for the vehicle behind to reduce before reversing

C. Allow a pedestrian or a passenger to assist you in directing you in reverse

D. Go round the roundabout again until you return to your exit

Answer = D

20) **You are driving on the right-hand lane of a two-way road. You turned right to another two-way road. In which position will you end up?**

A. Any of the lanes

B. The lane closest to the curb

C. The left-hand lane

D. All of the above

Answer = B

Chapter Eleven: **Sharing the Road**

1) **At which of the following time do road accidents occur?**

    A. At midnight

    B. At dusk

    C. At all time

    D. At dawn

Answer = C

2) **Which of the following is true about a truck and a passenger vehicle?**

    A. A truck traveling at the same speed as a passenger vehicle takes longer time to stop

    B. A passenger vehicle has longer stopping distance

    C. A truck can maneuver within a smaller space

    D. A truck has a smaller turning radius

Answer = A

3) While driving on the street, which of the following road users should a driver be most alert to?

   A. Oncoming vehicles

   B. Pedestrians crossing between parked cars

   C. Following vehicles

   D. A vehicle emerging from a side road

Answer = B

4) Which of the following location would you be extra careful and watchful for motorcyclists?

   A. At the bus stop

   B. At road junctions

   C. On the expressway

   D. When parking

Answer = B

5) **A driver making a right turn observed that a pedestrian was about crossing, what should he do?*****
   A. Wait for the pedestrian to finish crossing
   B. Honk for the pedestrian to wait
   C. continue turning, and the pedestrian will stop
   D. Signal to the pedestrian to cross

Answer = A

6) **Why should drivers look over their shoulder before making a turn into a side street?*****
   A. To balance properly before a turn
   B. They do not have a side mirror on that side
   C. To be sure of any road user at the blindspot
   D. It is an impulsive action

Answer = C

7) **You have parked on a narrow street. What should you do before exiting the car?**
   A. Honk to alert other road users

B. Open the door and step out

C. Look through the internal rear mirror to see the situation behind

D. Make sure no road user will be affected before you open the door

Answer = D

8) **Bicyclists are required to ride in the opposite direction of vehicles.**

A. True

B. False

Answer = B

9) **You are driving past a bicyclist. What should you do?*****

A. Flash your headlight

B. Honk at least once to alert the rider

C. Use the hazard light to alert following cars

D. Leave 3 feet space from the rider

Answer = D

10) **You were cut off by another driver while in traffic. What should you do?**

    A. Follow up with the driver immediately

    B. Join the next lane

    C. Ignore the driver

    D. Honk to warn the other driver

Answer = C

11) **Some drivers have the habit of driving very close to a vehicle in front of them. If you a face with the challenge of a vehicle following you as such, what should you do?**

    A. Speed up to widen the gap behind

    B. Slow down to widen the gap in front

    C. Signal the driver to overtake

    D. Steer to the next available free lane

Answer = B

12) **A driver is allowed to use one of the following lights at night when there is no**

indication that other road users would be affected by the light?

A. The full-beam headlight

B. The fog light

C. The dip light

D. The hazard light

Answer = A

13) **You will be embarking on a long journey in the early morning of Monday. Some friends invite you for a drink on Sunday evening. What should be your action?**

A. Take a few alcoholic drinks

B. Dilute your alcohol with water or lemon

C. Take enough food to avoid getting drunk

D. Avoid taking any alcohol in the gathering

Answer = D

14) **How does alcohol affect your driving?**

A. It keeps you awake

B. It gives you confidence on the road

C. It affects your judgment

D. It reduces drowsiness

Answer = C

15) **What should you do when there is an emergency vehicle with a blue flashing light behind?**

   A. Speed up your vehicle

   B. Look for the closest safe place and pull over

   C. Proceed until you are told to pull over

   D. Slow down for the vehicle to pass

Answer = B

16) **You are heading towards under a flyover that does not have a sidewalk. What should you do?**

   A. Drive while maintaining a designated speed

   B. Honk as you approach under the bridge

   C. Slow down and pass carefully

   D. Use your headlight for more visibility

Answer = C

17) **When driving on a narrow road that has no sidewalk, how are pedestrian suppose to walk?**

A. In the center of the road

B. By the side of the road that traffic is moving

C. By the side of the road but facing oncoming traffic

D. Any direction where traffic is less

Answer = C

18) **You saw a pedestrian on the road from a few feet about to cross the road. If there is no sidewalk at that location, what should you do?**

A. Slow down and stop for the pedestrian to finish crossing

B. Honk to put the pedestrian on alert and proceed

C. Continue with your journey while flashing your headlight

D. Caution the pedestrian for crossing at an inappropriate location

Answer = A

19) You looked through your side mirror to see a fire engine approaching. What should you do?

A. Speed up to the next street

B. Continue with your driving

C. Use your hazard light immediately

D. Pull over at the nearest safe side road

Answer = D

20) Which of the following should you be careful of when driving on a narrow road with cars parked by the sides of the road?

A. Sudden car door opening

B. Pedestrians coming ahead

C. Pedestrians coming behind

D. The state of the road

Answer = A

21) **You drove to a point where you found a pedestrian with a white cane attempting to cross the street. What should you do?**

   A. Sound your horn

   B. Stop for the pedestrian to cross

   C. Flash your light and proceed with your trip

   D. Wave for the pedestrian to cross

Answer = B

22) **How do you pass a cyclist on the road?**

   A. Accelerate pass

   B. Drive closer to the cyclist while passing

   C. Sound your horn before passing

   D. Slow down and pass, giving enough room

Answer = D

23) **Your car broke down on a highway, what should you do?**

   A. Step out and direct traffic from behind

   B. Keep your headlight on to indicate your stationary position

C. Stay in the car while waiting for help from the police

D. Turn on your four-way flashers (hazard light) to warn motorists

Answer = D

24) **You notice while driving that you need a rest, but the next service area is far away, which of the following is the best action to take?**

A. Find a safe place to stop

B. Move to the hard shoulder and park with your hazard light on

C. Check for a spacious central reserve and park

D. Look for a slip road and pull up

Answer = A

25) **When following another vehicle at night on an unlit road, which light should you use when you are 300ft behind the vehicle?*****

A. Dimed light

B. Full beam light

C. Headlight off

D. Flashing light and inner light

Answer = A

26) **If you see a pedestrian with a white cane that has a red tip, what readily comes to mind?**

A. The pedestrian has a hearing problem

B. The pedestrian is disabled

C. The pedestrian is blind

D. The pedestrian could be a street guard

Answer = C

27) **An emergency vehicle has passed you. How should you follow?**

A. Follow up immediately behind the vehicle

B. Follow not less than 300 feet behind

C. Drive to another lane to avoid the vehicle

D. Wait for two more vehicles to pass before you can join

Answer = B

28) **Lack of sleep has the following effect on the body?**
   A. Same effect as frustration
   B. Same effect as bottled anger
   C. Same result as alcohol
   D. None of the above

Answer = C

29) **You found yourself in danger of being hit by another vehicle moving towards you. What should you do?**
   A. Signal the driver to stop
   B. Flash your emergency light
   C. Flash your headlight constantly
   D. Sound your horn

Answer = D

30) **Which of the following location would you be extra careful and watchful for motorcyclists?**

A. At the bus stop

B. At a road junctions

C. On the motorway

D. When parking

Answer = B

31) **In which of the following situation does a blind person legally have the right of way when crossing the street?*****

A. When led by a dog and holding a white cane

B. When with a handkerchief

C. When helped by another person

D. When using dark glasses

Answer = A

32) **A driver is driving aggressively behind you. What should you do to avoid the driver hitting you?**

A. Pull to another lane

B. Use your hazard light

C. Use your horn

D. Signal him to calm down

Answer = A

33) **Your tire had blown out on your trip. What should you do?**

A. Drive to the nearest repair shop

B. Continue driving until you get to the nearest fueling station

C. Allow the car slow to a stop while holding firm the steering

D. Apply the brake

Answer = C

34) **To avoid a crash due to drowsy driving, teenagers should have a minimum of:**

A. 6 hours of sleep

B. 7 hours of sleep

C. 8 hours of sleep

D. 9 hours of sleep

Answer = C

35) **How long does it take the body to process alcohol in the body for an average person?**
    A. 60 minutes
    B. 70 minutes
    C. 80 minutes
    D. 90 minutes

Answer = A

36) **If a school bus with a flashing red light stops in from of you in the same lane, what should you do? *****
    A. Pass using another lane
    B. Stop for the bus
    C. Sound your horn for the driver to clear
    D. Sound your horn to alert the student

Answer = B

37) **A driver complained that he could not see correctly due to the blindspot. What does this mean?**

   A. He could not see the area not covered by the vehicle side mirrors

   B. He could not see because the area was out of his view

   C. He could not see the area outside the headlight beam

   D. He could not see due to minor eye defect in one of his eyes

Answer = A

38) **You are driving behind a large vehicle, but you cannot see any of the side mirrors. What does this indicate?**

   A. The front vehicle's side mirrors must have been missing

   B. The driver must have closed the side mirrors

   C. You are driving in the centerline of the large vehicle

D. You are too close to the vehicle

Answer = D

39) **Which of the following do blind pedestrians rely upon when crossing the road?*****

A. The sound in the environment

B. The color of your vehicle

C. The sound of your vehicle

D. The traffic signals and markings

Answer = C

40) **It is essential to stop your vehicle:**

A. 3 feet within the crosswalk

B. 5 feet within the crosswalk

C. 7 feet within the crosswalk

D. 9 feet within the crosswalk

Answer = B

41) When a pedestrian with a cane pulls the cane in and step out of the road, what should you do?***

   A. Stop and wait for the blind pedestrian to cross the road

   B. Wait and sound your horn for the blind pedestrian to cross the road

   C. Continue with your driving because the blind pedestrian is not ready to cross

   D. The blind pedestrian is prepared to cross the road

Answer = C

42) You are driving a hybrid car, which of the following road users should you must pay the most attention?

   A. A blind pedestrian

   B. A motorcyclist

   C. A bicyclist

   D. A pedestrian

Answer = A

43) **You drove to a crosswalk with pedestrians waiting to cross, what should you do?**

    A. Turn on your hazard light while crossing

    B. Sound your horn while passing

    C. Stop and signal the pedestrians to cross

    D. Stop and wait for the pedestrians to cross

Answer = D

44) **It is vital to give blind pedestrians verbal instructions when you want them to cross.**

    A. True

    B. False

Answer = B

45) **It is right to stop in the middle of a crosswalk.**

    A. True

    B. False

Answer = B

46) You are about turning when you saw a pedestrian waiting to cross. What should you do?***

A. Do nothing and proceed with your turning
B. Stop and instruct the pedestrian to cross
C. Sound your horn and instruct the pedestrian to cross
D. Wait for the pedestrian to cross

Answer = D

47) Why is it wrong to honk at blind persons?

A. They will not hear you
B. They do not care if you are honking for them
C. They have no idea whom the honking is for
D. They cannot tell your distance

Answer = C

48) It is right to park at a crosswalk.

A. True
B. False

Answer = B

49) **Which of the following is not correct in a work zone?**

    A. Watch out for work zone speed limit
    B. Watch out for speed limit warning sign
    C. Watch out for national speed sign
    D. Watch out for flaggers

Answer = C

50) **Which of the following should you not do at a construction zone?**

    A. Prepare to stop along the route
    B. Be ready to yield for a construction equipment
    C. Ignore instructions from flagger
    D. Avoid crossing the cones or barrier at the construction site

Answer = C

51) **While within a work zone with a narrow lane and closed shoulder, which of the**

following road users should you pay great attention?

A. Cyclists and pedestrians

B. Heavy equipment

C. Construction vehicles

D. Oncoming vehicles

Answer = A

52) **Which of the following do you expect to find while driving in a work zone?**

A. Functional traffic light

B. A wider driving area

C. Police and soldier directing traffic flow

D. Sudden slowing, stopping and changing of lanes

Answer = D

53) **You received a telephone call while driving within a work zone, what should you do?**

A. Receive the call and drive carefully

B. Use your hands-free to receive the call

C. Wait until you park outside the work zone before accepting the call

D. Receive the call using the speakout

Answer = C

54) **Which of the following is not a significant distractor while driving on the road?**

A. Listening to music

B. Texting while driving

C. Answering telephone call on wheels

D. Operating the GPS

Answer = A

55) **Anyone convicted of assaulting a highway worker can receive a fine or imprisonment.**

A. True

B. False

Answer = A

56) **A driver can stop temporarily to watch activities in a work zone.**

A. True

B. False

Answer = B

57) Why is there a double-fine-zone?

    A. To get more revenue from road users

    B. To discourage drivers from using a particular road

    C. To reduce the high rate of collision within the zone

    D. To make pedestrian use the road more

Answer = C

58) Which of the following is an example of a double-fine-zone?

    A. Less busy highways

    B. Streets

    C. Moderate traffic areas

    D. Highway construction zones

Answer = D

59) You saw an emergency vehicle ahead with an amber flashing light on your lane of a highway, what should you do?

A. Stop at the emergency area

B. Stop before you get to the emergency area

C. Flash your headlight

D. Move over to another lane

Answer = D

60) A person of 21 years or older should not have an Alcoholic Blood Concentration (BAC) of ....and more. ***

A. 0.05%

B. 0.065%

C. 0.08%

D. 0.10%

Answer = A

61) How many days do you have to notify DMV if you sell or transfer your vehicle?***

A. 14 days

B. 10 days

C. 7 days

D. 5 days

Answer D

62) **Unless a traffic sign denotes No U-turn, you may make a U-turn at which of these locations?**

A. On a one-way street

B. At an intersection that has the green light

C. At a railway crossing

D. At a two way road with central barrier

Answer = B

63) **Always moving from one lane to the other in a freeway during heavy traffic:**

A. Reduces the consumption of fuel

B. Helps to achieve better clearance ahead

C. Causes more congestion

D. Improves the traffic situation

Answer = C

64) **Which of the following passenger will need a child restraint?*****

A. A child of seven years old, four feet and seven inches tall

B. A passenger of eight years, four feet and eight inches tall

C. A passenger of six years, four feet and nine inches tall

D. A child of eight and a half years and five feet

Answer = A

65) **At which of these circumstances can you turn right when there is a solid red light showing? *****

A. Under no circumstances

B. After checking that there is no traffic

C. After stopping, unless otherwise posted

D. When the right turn light shows red

Answer = C

66) **Which action will you take if you see the sign below as you drive on the major road?**

A. Release the acceleration

B. Continue with your speed

C. Turn right

D. Turn left

Answer = D

67) **If you share the road with a light rail vehicle, what should you do?**

A. Pay no attention to the light rail vehicle

B. You cross in front of the light rail vehicle

C. Avoid driving next to a light rail vehicle

D. Carefully monitor the traffic signals because they can be interrupted by light rail vehicles

Answer = D

68) **At what time should you use the headlight?**

A. At dusk

B. When you cannot see 50 feet ahead

C. Anytime you find it difficult seeing others, or you cannot be seen

D. At one hour before dusk and an hour after dawn

Answer = C

69) **At what point does the road become most slippery?*****

A. After the rain

B. A few minutes into the rainfall

C. After it has rained heavily

D. Under a heavy sun

Answer = B

70) **It is illegal to smoke inside a vehicle with a passenger less than eighteen years old.*****

A. True

B. False

Answer = A

71) **When should you not pass another vehicle?**

A. When driving on a freeway with other vehicles behind you

B. Where pedestrians could cross the road

C. On an expressway

D. On a street with more than one lane

Answer = B

72) **You are driving on a highway, and there is a large vehicle in front of you. You should:**

A. Pull back to have a better view of the road ahead

B. Follow up closely

C. Drive at the hard shoulder to have a better view

D. Use your headlight for visibility

Answer = A

73) **When on the freeway, which of the following lanes is for only fast-moving vehicles?**

    A. The far-right lane

    B. The middle lant

    C. The far left lane

    D. All of the above

Answer = C

74) **You need to turn left on a two-way road. Where should you position before turning?**

    A. The right-hand lane

    B. Between the right-hand lane and the left-hand lane

    C. The left-hand lane

Answer = C

75) **You are driving on a freeway. What should be your maximum speed limit?**

    A. The speed as indicated in the dashboard

    B. The speed that makes you most comfortable

C. The average speed of the vehicles moving in your direction

D. The speed limited posted for the road

Answer = D

76) **Which of the following vehicle is not entitled for the entire lane of a roadway?**

A. Motorcycle

B. Car

C. Bus

D. None of the above

Answer = C

77) **What type of line is used to separate vehicles traveling in the opposite direction in which no vehicle is permitted to cross the line?**

A. Solid yellow line

B. Solid white line

C. Broken yellow line

D. Broken white line

Answer = A

78) **Motorcyclists have the same right and responsibilities as other motorists. *****
   A. True
   B. False

Answer = A

79) **Which of the following is the effect of a slow-moving vehicle driving on a fast-moving lane?**
   A. It makes other following vehicles to maintain a steady speed
   B. It could lead to a collision on the road
   C. It reduces the rate of accidents on the road
   D. None of the above

Answer = B

80) **What is the color of the road signs for road work ahead or road equipment ahead?**

A. Yellow

B. White

C. Orange

D. Red

Answer = C

81) **When changing lane, you must always use your turn signal.**

    A. True

    B. False

Answer = A

82) **Alcohol test, urine test, or breath test is mandatory for anyone who drives a motor vehicle in Florida.**

    A. True

    B. False

Answer = A

83) **If your medication makes you drowsy, when can you drive in such a condition?**

A. When a physician permits it

B. When the journey is less than one hour

C. If the weather is favorable

D. under no condition

Answer = D

84) **You need to make a right turn, and this will make you drive on the bicycle lane. How long are you permitted to drive on a bicycle lane before turning right?*****

A. 100 feet before the turn

B. 200 feet before the turn

C. 250 feet before the turn

D. 150 feet before the turn

Answer = B

85) **If your telephone rings while you are on steering wheels, what must you do?**

A. Allow it go to voice mail

B. Receive the call briefly

C. Infor the caller you are driving

D. Slow down, drive carefully and receive the call

Answer = A

86) Any bicycle used when it is dark should have the following?

A. Yellow flashing light

B. A red brake light

C. A rear tail-light and front headlight

D. A rear flashing light

Answer = C

87) When at a work zone, which of the following distances should you maintain?

A. Double the normal following distance

B. Maintain the normal following distance

C. Stay closer to the front vehicle

D. Cruise through the work zone

Answer = A

88) **A long vehicle driver is signaling right close to a crossroad but is moving to the left-hand side. What should you do?**

A. Pass through the right-hand side

B. Stop by the right-hand side

C. Overtake through the right-hand side

D. Wait for the vehicle to finish its turning

Answer = D

89) **A fluorescent or a reflective orange triangle on a red border is the color emblem of:**

A. Loaded vehicles

B. Emergency vehicles

C. Slow-moving vehicles

D. Animals on the street

Answer = C

90) **You can cause congestion on the road when you drive your car too slowly.**

A. True

B. False

Answer = A

Made in the USA
Columbia, SC
16 November 2020

24694934R00104